SMOKER GRILL PARTY RECIPES

The Ultimate BBQ Cookbook. Light and Tasty Recipes for Parties with Family and Friends

Mark Pit

The information in the following pages is broadly considered a truthful and accurate account of facts and as such, any inattention, use, or misuse of the information in question by the reader will render any resulting actions solely under their purview. There are no scenarios in which the publisher or the original author of this work can be in any fashion deemed liable for any hardship or damages that may befall them after undertaking information described herein.

Additionally, the information in the following pages is intended only for informational purposes and should thus be thought of as universal. As befitting its nature, it is presented without assurance regarding its prolonged validity or interim quality. Trademarks that are mentioned are done without written consent and can in no way be considered an endorsement from the trademark holder.

Summary

—

Introduction

A Smoker barbecue is an ideal product for those who want to give a smoky flavor to their dishes without getting their hands excessively dirty with charcoal or firewood. For those who don't want to deal with the inconvenience of temperature control or subsequent cleaning, but love the taste of dishes cooked over a flame. Pellet grills also offer the convenience of combining several cooking options in one unit. While it may not be able to reach the same temperatures as charcoal, it still manages to heat up the griddle or grill in a matter of minutes, making it always ready to use in much less time than it takes to prepare barbecue charcoal.

There are many grills available in the market that you can invest in for your outdoor cooking. These innovative grills allow you to cook authentic grilled food. However, they don't deviate from the tradition of cooking using wood pellets, so you don't get that nasty aftertaste you get from cooking in a gas grill.

These types of smoker grills are known for cooking food using all-natural wood pellets so that the food smells and tastes great and healthy. The best ones have a motor that spins the auger thus constantly feeding the burn pot, so you can get even cooking.

Pellet grills give you even more, as if that weren't enough. With your new pellet grill, you have the absolute convenience of combining multiple cooking options. Old-time smokers only smoke their food, so if you want to grill, bake, and roast your food, you should purchase separate units for each process.

Pellet grills are different from propane or gas grills in that they offer more control. Pellet grills and gas grills both offer their own set of convenient features for the outdoor cook, but look closer, and you'll see some big differences. Gas grills are very good when cooking chores, but due to poor insulation, they generally don't perform very well at all low cooking temperatures. Also, the older style of propane grills need to be set up to receive the right amount of ventilation. This alone makes them a poor choice for smokers. The pellet grill is a must-have choice in today's world!

Pellet grills provide the chef with more flavor options. With pellet grills, wood pellets come in many flavors. This provides you with the ability to cook all foods on your Pellet Smoker Grill. In the end, sure, they both cook food, but the pellet grill is exponentially better on so many levels. For me, there is no other choice but the Pellet Smoker Grill!

Then there's whether to use a pellet grill or stick with the highly coveted charcoal method of barbecuing your fine foods.

Charcoal grills have long been considered the king of the backyard barbecue area. There are several choices of charcoal grill configurations, but with two choices for fuel: charcoal or charcoal briquettes. Grilling using a charcoal grill is definitely a labor of love. I know several people who defend them to the bitter end, and that's okay. We're different, and thank goodness for that, too. However, cooking on a charcoal grill is not that easy. It takes a lot of practice to get all the elements just right, and it's hard to control the temperatures.

Pellet grills for grilling and smoking are infinitely easier. This is exactly why they have become the number one seller in the nation. As far as cleaning goes, have you ever seen a charcoal grill the morning after? You may need to take them out to the trash or recycling. It's not the same with a pellet grill though!

1   Cajun Chicken Breasts

Preparation Time: 10 Minutes

Cooking Time: 6 Hours

Servings: 6

Ingredients:

- 2 lb. skinless, boneless chicken breasts
- 2 tbsp. Cajun seasoning
- 1 C. BBQ sauce

Directions:

1.   Set the temperature of Traeger Grill to 225 degrees F and preheat with a closed lid for 15 mins.

2.   Rub the chicken breasts with Cajun seasoning generously.

3.   Put the chicken breasts onto the grill and cook for about 4-6 hours.

4.   During the last hour of cooking, coat the breasts with BBQ sauce twice.

5.   Serve hot.

Nutrition:

Calories per serving: 252

Carbohydrates: 15.1g

Protein: 33.8g

Fat: 5.5g

Sugar: 10.9g

Sodium: 570mg

Fiber: 0.3g

2   BBQ Sauce Smothered Chicken Breasts

Preparation Time: 15 Minutes

Cooking Time: 30 Minutes

Servings: 4

Ingredients:

- 1 tsp. garlic, crushed
- 2 tbsp. spicy BBQ sauce
- ¼ C. olive oil
- 1 tbsp. sweet mesquite seasoning
- 1 tbsp. Worcestershire sauce
- Four chicken breasts
- 2 tbsp. regular BBQ sauce
- 2 tbsp. honey bourbon BBQ sauce

Directions:

1.   Set the temperature of Traeger Grill to 450 degrees F and preheat with a closed lid for 15 mins.

2.   In a large bowl, mix garlic, oil, Worcestershire sauce, and mesquite seasoning.

3.   Brush chicken breasts with seasoning mixture evenly.

4.   Place the chicken breasts onto the grill and cook for about 20-30 mins.

5.   In the meantime, in a bowl, mix all 3 BBQ sauces.

6.   In the last 4-5 mins of cooking, coat the breast with BBQ sauce mixture.

7.   Serve hot.

Nutrition:

Calories per serving: 421

Carbohydrates: 10.1g

Protein: 41.2g

Fat: 23.3g

Sugar: 6.9g

Sodium: 763mg

Fiber: 0.2g

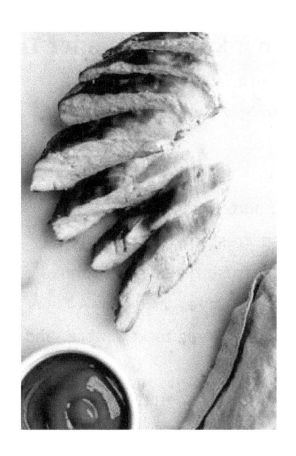

3   Thanksgiving Dinner Turkey

Preparation Time: 15 Minutes

Cooking Time: 4 Hours

Servings: 16

Ingredients:

- ☐   ½ lb. butter, softened
- ☐   2 tbsp. fresh thyme, chopped
- ☐   2 tbsp. fresh rosemary, chopped
- ☐   Six garlic cloves, crushed
- ☐   1 (20-lb.) whole turkey, neck, and giblets removed
- ☐   Salt and freshly ground black pepper

Directions:

1.   Set the temperature of Traeger Grill to 300 degrees F and preheat with closed lid for 15 mins, using charcoal.

2.   Place butter, fresh herbs, garlic, salt, and black pepper and mix well in a bowl.

3.   With your fingers, separate the turkey skin from the breast to create a pocket.

4.   Stuff the breast pocket with a ¼-inch thick layer of the butter mixture.

5.   Season the turkey with salt and black pepper evenly.

6.   Arrange the turkey onto the grill and cook for 3-4 hours.

7.   Remove the turkey from the grill and place onto a cutting board for about 15-20 mins before carving.

8.   With a sharp knife, cut the turkey into desired-sized pieces and serve.

Nutrition:

Calories per serving: 965

Carbohydrates: 0.6g

Protein: 106.5g

Fat: 52g

Sugar: 0g

Sodium: 1916mg

Fiber: 0.2g

4   Perfectly Smoked Turkey Legs

Preparation Time: 15 Minutes

Cooking Time: 4 Hours

Servings: 6

Ingredients:

For Turkey:

- 3 tbsp. Worcestershire sauce
- 1 tbsp. canola oil
- Six turkey legs

For Rub:

- ¼ C. chipotle seasoning
- 1 tbsp. brown sugar
- 1 tbsp. paprika

For Sauce:

- 1 C. white vinegar
- 1 tbsp. canola oil
- 1 tbsp. chipotle BBQ sauce

Directions:

1.   For turkey in a bowl, add the Worcestershire sauce and canola oil and mix well.

2.   With your fingers, loosen the skin of legs.

3.   With your fingers, coat the legs under the skin with an oil mixture.

4.   In another bowl, mix rub ingredients.

5.   Rub the spice mixture under and the outer surface of turkey legs generously.

6.   Transfer the legs into a large sealable bag and refrigerate for about 2-4 hours.

7.   Remove the refrigerator's turkey legs and set aside at room temperature for at least 30 mins before cooking.

8.   Set the temperature of Traeger Grill to 200-220 degrees F and preheat with a closed lid for 15 mins.

9.   In a small pan, mix all sauce ingredients on low heat and cook until warmed thoroughly, stirring continuously.

10.   Place the turkey legs onto the grill cook for about 3½-4 hours, coating with sauce after every 45 mins.

11.   Serve hot.

Nutrition:

Calories per serving: 430

Carbohydrates: 4.9g

Protein: 51.2g

Fat: 19.5g

Sugar: 3.9g

Sodium: 1474mg

Fiber: 0.5g

5   Texas-Style Brisket Rub

Preparation Time: 5 Minutes

Cooking Time: 10 Minutes

Servings: 1

Ingredients:

- 2 tsp Sugar
- 2 Tbsp Kosher salt
- 2 tsp Chili powder
- 2 Tbsp Black pepper
- 2 Tbsp Cayenne pepper
- 2 Tbsp Powdered garlic
- 2 tsp Grounded cumin
- 2 Tbsp Powdered onion
- 1/4 cup paprika, smoked

Directions:

1.   Mix all the ingredients in a small bowl until it is well blended.

2.   Transfer to an airtight jar or container. Store in a cool place.

Nutrition:

Calories: 18kcal

Carbs: 2g

Fat: 1g

Protein: 0.6g

6   Pork Dry Rub

Preparation Time: 5 Minutes

Cooking Time: 10 Minutes

Servings: 1 Cup

Ingredients:

- 1 Tbsp Kosher salt
- 2 Tbsp Powered onions
- 1 Tbsp Cayenne pepper
- 1 tsp Dried mustard
- 1/4 cup brown sugar
- 1 Tbsp Powdered garlic
- 1 Tbsp Powdered chili pepper
- 1/4 cup smoked paprika
- 2 Tbsp Black pepper

Directions:

1.   Combine all the ingredients in a small bowl.

2.   Transfer to an airtight jar or container.

3.   Keep stored in a cool, dry place.

Nutrition:

Calories: 16kcal   Carbs: 3g

Fat:0.9g   Protein: 0.8g

7   Texas Barbeque Rub

Preparation Time: 5 Minutes

Cooking Time: 10 Minutes

Servings: ½ cup

Ingredients:

- 1 tsp Sugar
- 1 Tbsp Seasoned salt
- 1 Tbsp Black pepper
- 1 tsp Chili powder
- 1 Tbsp Powdered onions
- 1 Tbsp Smoked paprika
- 1 tsp Sugar
- 1 Tbsp Powdered garlic

Directions:

1. Pour all the ingredients into a small bowl and mix thoroughly.

2. Keep stored in an airtight jar or container.

Nutrition:

Calories: 22kcal

Carbs: 2g

Fat: 0.2g

Protein: 0.6g

8   Barbeque Sauce

Preparation Time: 5 Minutes

Cooking Time: 10 Minutes

Servings: 2 Cups

Ingredients:

- 1/4 cup of water
- 1/4 cup red wine vinegar
- 1 Tbsp Worcestershire sauce
- 1 tsp Paprika
- 1 tsp Salt
- Tbsp Dried mustard
- 1 tsp black pepper
- 1 cup ketchup
- 1 cup brown sugar

Directions:

1.   Pour all the ingredients into a food processor, one after the other.

2.   Process until they are evenly mixed.

3.   Transfer sauce to a close lid jar. Store in the refrigerator.

Nutrition:

Calories: 43kcal

Carbs: 10g

Fat: 0.3g

Protein: 0.9g

9   Steak Sauce

Preparation Time: 5 Minutes

Cooking Time: 20 Minutes

Servings: ½ Cup

Ingredients:

- 1 Tbsp Malt vinegar
- 1/2 tsp Salt
- 1/2 tsp black pepper
- 1 Tbsp Tomato sauce
- 2 Tbsp brown sugar
- 1 tsp hot pepper sauce
- 2 Tbsp Worcestershire sauce
- 2 Tbsp Raspberry jam.

Directions:

1.   Preheat your grill for indirect cooking at 150°F

2.   Place a saucepan over grates, add all your ingredients, and allow to boil.

3.   Reduce the temperature to Smoke and allow the sauce to simmer for 10 minutes or until sauce is thick.

Nutrition:

Calories: 62.1kcal

Carbs: 15.9g

Fat: 0.3g

Protein:0.1g

10 Bourbon Whiskey Sauce

Preparation Time: 20 Minutes

Cooking Time: 25 Minutes

Servings: 3 Cups

Ingredients:

- 2 cups ketchup
- 1/4 cup Worcestershire sauce
- 3/4 cup bourbon whiskey
- 1/3 cup apple cider vinegar
- 1/2 onions, minced
- 1/4 cup of tomato paste
- 2 cloves of garlic, minced
- 1/2 tsp Black pepper
- 1/2 cup brown sugar
- 1/2 Tbsp Salt
- Hot pepper sauce to taste
- 1 Tbsp Liquid smoke flavoring

Directions:

1. Preheat your grill for indirect cooking at 150°F

2. Place a saucepan over grates, then add the whiskey, garlic, and onions.

3.   Simmer until the onion is translucent. Then add the other ingredients and adjust the temperature to Smoke. Simmer for 20 minutes. For a smooth sauce, sieve.

Nutrition:

Calories: 107kcal

Carbs:16.6g

Fat: 1.8g

Protein:0.8g

11   Chicken Marinade

Preparation Time: 5 Minutes

Cooking Time: 30 Minutes

Servings: 3 Cups

Ingredients:

☐   halved chicken breast (bone and skin removed)

☐   1 Tbsp Spicy brown mustard

☐   2/3 cup of soy sauce

☐   1 tsp Powdered garlic

☐   2 Tbsp Liquid smoke flavoring

☐   2/3 cup extra virgin olive oil

☐   2/3 cup lemon juice

☐   2 tsp Black pepper

Directions:

1.   Mix all the ingredients in a large bowl.

2.   Pour the chicken into the bowl and allow it to marinate for about 3-4hours in the refrigerator. Remove the chicken, then smoke, grill, or roast the chicken.

Nutrition:

Calories: 507kcal

Carbs:46.6g

Fat: 41.8g

Protein: 28g

12 Carne Asada Marinade

Preparation Time: 30 Minutes

Cooking Time: 1 Hour and 30 Minutes

Servings: 5 Cups111

Ingredients:

- 2 cloves garlic, chopped
- 1 tsp Lemon juice
- 1/2 cup extra virgin olive oil
- 1/2 tsp Salt
- 1/2 tsp Pepper

Directions:

1. Mix all your ingredients in a bowl.

2. Pour the beef into the bowl and allow to marinate for 2-3hours before grilling.

Nutrition:

Calories: 465kcal

Carbs: 26g

Fat: 15g

Protein: 28g

13 Grapefruit Juice Marinade

Preparation Time: 25 Minutes

Cooking Time: 35 Minutes

Servings: 3 Cups

Ingredients:

- 1/2 reduced-sodium soy sauce
- 3 cups grapefruit juice, unsweetened
- 1-1/2 lb. Chicken, bone and skin removed
- 1/4 brown sugar

Directions:

1. Thoroughly mix all your ingredients in a large bowl.

2. Add the chicken and allow it to marinate for 2-3 hours before grilling.

Nutrition:

Calories: 489kcal

Carbs: 21.3g

Fat: 12g

Protein: 24g

14 Steak Marinade

Preparation Time: 5 Minutes

Cooking Time: 10 Minutes

Servings: 2 Cups

Ingredients:

- 1 Tbsp Worcestershire sauce
- 2 Tbsp Red wine vinegar
- 1/2 cup barbeque sauce
- 3 Tbsp soy sauce
- 1/4 cup steak sauce
- 1 clove garlic (minced)
- 1 tsp Mustard
- Pepper and salt to taste

Directions:

1. Pour all the ingredients in a bowl and mix thoroughly.

2. Use immediately or keep refrigerated.

Nutrition:

Calories: 303kcal

Carbs: 42g

Fat: 10g

Protein:2.4g

15 Dry Rub for Ribs

Preparation Time: 10 Minutes

Cooking Time: 0 Minutes

Servings: 8

Ingredients:

- three tablespoons brown sugar
- One and a half tablespoons paprika
- One and a half tablespoons salt
- one teaspoon garlic powder
- One and a half tablespoons ground black pepper

Directions:

1. Combine black pepper, brown sugar, salt, paprika, and garlic powder. Now, rub into the pork ribs. Let ribs to marinate whole night and then grill as you want.

Nutrition:

Calories: 16kcal

Carbs: 3g

Fat:0.9g

Protein: 0.8g

16 Special BBQ Sauce

Preparation Time: 10 Minutes

Cooking Time: 0 Minutes

Servings: 32

Ingredients:

- One and half cups brown sugar
- One and a half cups ketchup
- one tablespoon Worcestershire sauce
- Two and a half tablespoons dry mustard
- Two teaspoons paprika
- Two teaspoons salt
- Half cup red wine vinegar
- Half cup waters
- One and a half teaspoons black pepper
- Two dashes hot pepper sauce

Directions:

- Take a blender; merge Worcestershire sauce, vinegar, brown sugar, water, and ketchup. Now, season with hot pepper sauce, paprika, mustard, pepper, and salt. Mix until it gets smooth.

Nutrition:

Calories: 43kcal

Carbs: 10g

Fat: 0.3g

Protein: 0.9g

17 Special Teriyaki Marinade

Preparation Time: 10 Minutes

Cooking Time: 0 Minutes

Servings: 24

Ingredients:

- one cup soy sauce
- one cup water
- ¾ cup white sugar
- ¼ cup Worcestershire sauce
- three tablespoons distilled white vinegar
- three tablespoons vegetable oil
- one teaspoon grated fresh ginger
- 1/3 cup dried onion flakes
- two teaspoons garlic powder

Directions:

1.   Take an intermediate bowl and combine sugar, onions, ginger, water, Worcestershire sauce, soy sauce, garlic powder, vinegar, and oil. Now, stir well until sugar dissolves completely

Nutrition:

Calories: 465kcal

Carbs: 26g

Fat: 15g

Protein: 28g

18 Grilled Pineapple with Chocolate Sauce

Preparation Time: 10 Minutes

Cooking Time: 25 Minutes

Servings: 8

Ingredients:

- 1pineapple
- 8 oz bittersweet chocolate chips
- 1/2 cup spiced rum
- 1/2 cup whipping cream
- 2tbsp light brown sugar

Directions:

1.   Preheat pellet grill to 400°F.

2.   De-skin, the pineapple, then slice the pineapple into 1 in cubes.

3.   In a saucepan, combine chocolate chips. When chips begin to melt, add rum to the saucepan. Continue to stir until combined, then add a splash of the pineapple's juice.

4.   Add in whipping cream and continue to stir the mixture. Once the sauce is smooth and thickening, lower heat to simmer to keep warm.

5.   Thread pineapple cubes onto skewers. Sprinkle skewers with brown sugar.

6.   Place skewers on the grill grate. Grill for about 5 minutes per side, or until grill marks begin to develop.

7.   Remove skewers from grill and allow to rest on a plate for about 5 minutes. Serve alongside warm chocolate sauce for dipping.

Nutrition:

Calories: 112.6

Fat: 0.5 g

Cholesterol: 0

Carbohydrate: 28.8 g

Fiber: 1.6 g

Sugar: 0.1 g

Protein: 0.4 g

19 Nectarine and Nutella Sundae

Preparation Time: 10 Minutes

Cooking Time: 25 Minutes

Servings: 4

Ingredients:

- 2nectarines halved and pitted
- 2tsp honey
- 4tbsp Nutella
- 4scoops vanilla ice cream
- 1/4 cup pecans, chopped
- Whipped cream, to top
- 4cherries, to top

Directions:

1. Preheat pellet grill to 400°F.

2. Slice nectarines in half and remove the pits.

3. Brush the inside (cut side) of each nectarine half with honey.

4. Place nectarines directly on the grill grate, cut side down—Cook for 5-6 minutes, or until grill marks develop.

5. Flip nectarines and cook on the other side for about 2 minutes.

6. Remove nectarines from the grill and allow it to cool.

7. Fill the pit cavity on each nectarine half with 1 tbsp Nutella.

8. Place one scoop of ice cream on top of Nutella. Top with whipped cream, cherries, and sprinkle chopped pecans. Serve and enjoy!

Nutrition:

Calories: 90

Fat: 3 g

Carbohydrate: 15g

Sugar: 13 g

Protein: 2 g

20 Cinnamon Sugar Donut Holes

Preparation Time: 10 Minutes

Cooking Time: 35 Minutes

Servings: 4

Ingredients:

- [ ] 1/2 cup flour
- [ ] 1tbsp cornstarch
- [ ] 1/2 tsp baking powder
- [ ] 1/8 tsp baking soda
- [ ] 1/8 tsp ground cinnamon
- [ ] 1/2 tsp kosher salt
- [ ] 1/4 cup buttermilk
- [ ] 1/4 cup sugar
- [ ] 11/2 tbsp butter, melted
- [ ] 1egg
- [ ] 1/2 tsp vanilla
- [ ] Topping
- [ ] 2tbsp sugar
- [ ] 1tbsp sugar
- [ ] 1tsp ground cinnamon

Directions:

1. Preheat pellet grill to 350°F.

2.   In a medium bowl, combine flour, cornstarch, baking powder, baking soda, ground cinnamon, and kosher salt. Whisk to combine.

3.   In a separate bowl, combine buttermilk, sugar, melted butter, egg, and vanilla. Whisk until the egg is thoroughly combined.

4.   Pour wet mixture into the flour mixture and stir. Stir just until combined, careful not to overwork the mixture.

5.   Spray mini muffin tin with cooking spray.

6.   Spoon 1 tbsp of donut mixture into each mini muffin hole.

7.   Place the tin on the pellet grill grate and bake for about 18 minutes, or until a toothpick can come out clean.

8.   Remove muffin tin from the grill and let rest for about 5 minutes.

9.   In a small bowl, combine 1 tbsp sugar and 1 tsp ground cinnamon.

10.   Melt 2 tbsp of butter in a glass dish. Dip each donut hole in the melted butter, then mix

and toss with cinnamon sugar. Place completed donut holes on a plate to serve.

Nutrition:

Calories: 190

Fat: 17 g

Carbohydrate: 21 g

Fiber: 1 g

Sugar: 8 g

Protein: 3 g

21 Pellet Grill Chocolate Chip Cookies

Preparation Time: 20 Minutes

Cooking Time: 45 Minutes

Servings: 12

Ingredients:

- ☐ 1cup salted butter softened
- ☐ 1cup of sugar
- ☐ 1cup light brown sugar
- ☐ 2tsp vanilla extract
- ☐ 2large eggs
- ☐ 3cups all-purpose flour
- ☐ 1tsp baking soda
- ☐ 1/2 tsp baking powder
- ☐ 1tsp natural sea salt
- ☐ 2cups semi-sweet chocolate chips or chunks

Directions:

1. Preheat pellet grill to 375°F.

2. Line a large baking sheet with parchment paper and set aside.

3.   In a medium bowl, mix flour, baking soda, salt, and baking powder. Once combined, set aside.

4.   In stand mixer bowl, combine butter, white sugar, and brown sugar until combined. Beat in eggs and vanilla. Beat until fluffy.

5.   Mix in dry ingredients, continue to stir until combined.

6.   Add chocolate chips and mix thoroughly.

7.   Roll 3 tbsp of dough at a time into balls and place them on your cookie sheet. Evenly space them apart, with about 2-3 inches in between each ball.

8.   Place cookie sheet directly on the grill grate and bake for 20-25 minutes until the cookies' outside is slightly browned.

9.   Remove from grill and allow to rest for 10 minutes. Serve and enjoy!

Nutrition:

Calories: 120

Fat: 4

Cholesterol: 7.8 mg

Carbohydrate: 22.8 g

Fiber: 0.3 g

Sugar: 14.4 g

Protein: 1.4 g

22 Delicious Donuts on a Grill

Preparation Time: 5 Minutes

Cooking Time: 10 Minutes

Servings: 6

Ingredients:

- ☐ 1-1/2 cups sugar, powdered
- ☐ 1/3 cup whole milk
- ☐ 1/2 teaspoon vanilla extract
- ☐ 16 ounces of biscuit dough, prepared
- ☐ Oil spray, for greasing
- ☐ 1cup chocolate sprinkles, for sprinkling

Directions:

1. Take a medium bowl and mix sugar, milk, and vanilla extract.

2. Combine well to create a glaze.

3. Set the glaze aside for further use.

4. Place the dough onto the flat, clean surface.

5. Flat the dough with a rolling pin.

6. Use a ring mold, about an inch, and cut the hole in each round dough's center.

7. Place the dough on a plate and refrigerate for 10 minutes.

8.	Open the grill and install the grill grate inside it.

9.	Close the hood.

10.	Now, select the grill from the menu, and set the temperature to medium.

11.	Set the time to 6 minutes.

12.	Select start and begin preheating.

13.	Remove the dough from the refrigerator and coat it with cooking spray from both sides.

14.	When the unit beeps, the grill is preheated; place the adjustable amount of dough on the grill grate.

15.	Close the hood, and cook for 3 minutes.

16.	After 3 minutes, remove donuts and place the remaining dough inside.

17.	Cook for 3 minutes.

18.	Once all the donuts are ready, sprinkle chocolate sprinkles on top.

19.	Enjoy.

Nutrition:

Calories: 400

Total Fat: 11g

Cholesterol: 1mg

Sodium: 787mg

Total Carbohydrate: 71.3g

Dietary Fiber 0.9g

Total Sugars: 45.3g

Protein: 5.7g

23 Smoked Pumpkin Pie

Preparation Time: 10 Minutes

Cooking Time: 50 Minutes

Servings: 8

Ingredients:

- ☐ 1tbsp cinnamon
- ☐ 1-1/2 tbsp pumpkin pie spice
- ☐ 15oz can pumpkin
- ☐ 14oz can sweetened condensed milk
- ☐ 2beaten eggs
- ☐ 1unbaked pie shell
- ☐ Topping: whipped cream

Directions:

1. Preheat your smoker to 325oF.

2. Place a baking sheet, rimmed, on the smoker upside down, or use a cake pan.

3. Combine all your ingredients in a bowl, large, except the pie shell, then pour the mixture into a pie crust.

4. Place the pie on the baking sheet and smoke for about 50-60 minutes until a knife comes out clean when inserted. Make sure the center is set.

5.   Remove and cool for about 2 hours or refrigerate overnight.

6.   Serve with a whipped cream dollop and enjoy it!

Nutrition:

Calories: 292

Total Fat: 11g

Total Carbs: 42g

Protein: 7g

Sugars: 29g

Fiber: 5g

Sodium: 168mg

24 Wood Pellet Smoked Nut Mix

Preparation Time: 15 Minutes

Cooking Time: 20 Minutes

Servings: 12

Ingredients:

☐   3cups mixed nuts (pecans, peanuts, almonds, etc.)

☐   1/2 tbsp brown sugar

☐   1tbsp thyme, dried

☐   1/4 tbsp mustard powder

☐   1tbsp olive oil, extra-virgin

Directions:

1.   Preheat your pellet grill to 250oF with the lid closed for about 15 minutes.

2.   Combine all ingredients in a bowl, large, then transfer into a cookie sheet lined with parchment paper.

3.   Place the cookie sheet on a grill and grill for about 20 minutes.

4.   Remove the nuts from the grill and let cool.

5.   Serve and enjoy.

Nutrition:

Calories: 249

Total Fat: 21.5g

Saturated Fat: 3.5g

Total Carbs: 12.3g

Net Carbs: 10.1g

Protein: 5.7g

Sugars: 5.6g

Fiber: 2.1g

Sodium: 111mg

25 Grilled Peaches and Cream

Preparation Time: 15 Minutes

Cooking Time: 8 Minutes

Servings: 8

Ingredients:

- 4halved and pitted peaches
- 1tbsp vegetable oil
- 2tbsp clover honey
- 1cup cream cheese, soft with honey and nuts

Directions:

1. Preheat your pellet grill to medium-high heat.

2. Coat the peaches lightly with oil and place on the grill pit side down.

3. Grill for about 5 minutes until nice grill marks on the surfaces.

4. Turn over the peaches, then drizzle with honey.

5. Spread and cream cheese dollop where the pit was and grill for additional 2-3 minutes until the filling becomes warm.

6.　　Serve immediately.

Nutrition:

Calories: 139

Total Fat: 10.2g

Total Carbs: 11.6g

Protein: 1.1g

Sugars: 12g

Sodium: 135mg

26 Berry Cobbler on a Pellet Grill

Preparation Time: 15 Minutes

Cooking Time: 35 Minutes

Servings: 8

Ingredients:

For fruit filling

- 3cups frozen mixed berries
- 1lemon juice
- 1cup brown sugar
- 1tbsp vanilla extract
- 1bsp lemon zest, finely grated
- A pinch of salt

For cobbler topping

- 1-1/2 cups all-purpose flour
- 1-1/2 tbsp baking powder
- 3tbsp sugar, granulated
- 1/2 tbsp salt
- 8tbsp cold butter
- 1/2 cup sour cream
- 2tbsp raw sugar

Directions:

1.   Set your pellet grill on "smoke" for about 4-5 minutes with the lid open until fire establishes, and your grill starts smoking.

2.   Preheat your grill to 350 for about 10-15 minutes with the grill lid closed.

3.   Meanwhile, combine frozen mixed berries, Lemon juice, brown sugar, vanilla, lemon zest, and salt pinch. Transfer into a skillet and let the fruit sit and thaw.

4.   Mix flour, baking powder, sugar, and salt in a bowl, medium. Cut cold butter into peas sizes using a pastry blender, then add to the mixture. Stir to mix everything.

5.   Stir in sour cream until dough starts coming together.

6.   Pinch small pieces of dough and place over the fruit until fully covered. Splash the top with raw sugar.

7.   Now place the skillet directly on the grill grate, close the lid, cook for about 35 minutes

until juices bubble, and a golden-brown dough topping.

8.   Remove the skillet from the pellet grill and cool for several minutes.

9.   Scoop and serve warm.

Nutrition:

Calories: 371

Total Fat: 13g

Total Carbs: 60g

Protein: 3g

Sugars: 39g

Fiber: 2g

Sodium: 269mg

27 Pellet Grill Apple Crisp

Preparation Time: 20 Minutes

Cooking Time: 60 Minutes

Servings: 15

Ingredients:

- [ ] Apples
- [ ] Ten large apples
- [ ] 1/2 cup flour
- [ ] 1cup sugar, dark brown
- [ ] 1/2 tbsp cinnamon
- [ ] 1/2 cup butter slices
- [ ] Crisp
- [ ] 3cups oatmeal, old-fashioned
- [ ] 1-1/2 cups softened butter, salted
- [ ] 1-1/2 tbsp cinnamon
- [ ] 2cups brown sugar

Directions:

1. Preheat your grill to 350.

2. Wash, peel, core, and dice the apples into cubes, medium-size

3. Mix flour, dark brown sugar, and cinnamon, then toss with your apple cubes.

4.   Spray a baking pan, 10x13", with cooking spray, then place apples inside. Top with butter slices.

5.   Mix all crisp ingredients in a medium bowl until well combined. Place the mixture over the apples.

6.   Place on the grill and cook for about 1-hour checking after every 15-20 minutes to ensure cooking is even. Do not place it on the hottest grill part.

7.   Remove and let sit for about 20-25 minutes

8.   It's very warm.

Nutrition:

Calories: 528

Total Fat: 26g

Total Carbs: 75g

Protein: 4g

Sugars: 51g

Fiber: 5g

Sodium: 209mg

28 Fromage Macaroni and Cheese

Preparation Time: 30 Minutes

Cooking Time: 1 Hour

Servings: 8

Ingredients:

- ¼ c. all-purpose flour
- ½ stick butter
- Butter, for greasing
- One-pound cooked elbow macaroni
- One c. grated Parmesan
- 8 ounces cream cheese
- Two c. shredded Monterey Jack
- 3 t. garlic powder
- Two t. salt
- One t. pepper
- Two c. shredded Cheddar, divided
- Three c. milk

Directions:

1. Add the butter to a pot and melt. Mix in the flour. Stir constantly for a minute. Mix in the pepper, salt, garlic powder, and milk. Let it boil.

2.   After lowering the heat, let it simmer for about 5 mins, or until it has thickened. Remove from the heat.

3.   Mix in the cream cheese, parmesan, Monterey Jack, and 1 ½ c. of cheddar. Stir everything until melted. Fold in the pasta.

4.   Add wood pellets to your smoker and keep your cooker's startup procedure. Preheat your smoker, with your lid closed, until it reaches 225.

5.   Butter a 9" x 13" baking pan. Pour the macaroni mixture into the pan and lay on the grill. Cover and allow it to smoke for an hour, or until it has become bubbly. Top the macaroni with the rest of the cheddar during the last

6.   Serve.

Nutrition:

Calories: 180

Carbs: 19g

Fat: 8g

Protein: 8g

29 Spicy Barbecue Pecans

Preparation Time: 15 Minutes

Cooking Time: 1 Hour

Servings: 2

Ingredients:

- 2 ½ t. garlic powder
- 16 ounces raw pecan halves
- One t. onion powder
- One t. pepper
- Two t. salt
- One t. dried thyme
- Butter, for greasing
- 3 T. melted butter

Directions:

1. Add wood pellets to your smoker and follow your cooker's startup method.

2. Preheat your smoker, with your lid closed, until it reaches 225.

3. Cover and smoke for an hour, flipping the nuts one. Make sure the nuts are toasted and heated. They should be removed from the grill.

4. Set aside to cool and dry.

Nutrition:

Calories: 150

Carbs: 16g

Fat: 9g

Protein: 1g

30 Blackberry Pie

Preparation Time: 10 Minutes

Cooking Time: 40 Minutes

Servings: 8

Ingredients:

- ☐ Butter, for greasing
- ☐ ½ c. all-purpose flour
- ☐ ½ c. milk
- ☐ Two pints blackberries
- ☐ Two c. sugar, divided
- ☐ One box of refrigerated piecrusts
- ☐ One stick melted butter
- ☐ One stick of butter
- ☐ Vanilla ice cream

Directions:

1.   Add wood pellets to your smoker and follow your cooker's startup method.

2.   Preheat your smoker, with your lid closed, until it reaches 375.

3.   Unroll the second pie crust and lay it over the skillet.

4.   Lower the lid, then smoke for 15 to 20 minutes or until it is browned and bubbly.

5.   Serve the hot pie with some vanilla ice cream.

Nutrition:

Calories: 100

Carbs: 10g

Fat: 0g

Protein: 15g

31 S'mores Dip

Preparation Time: 0 Minutes

Cooking Time: 15 Minutes

Servings: 6-8

Ingredients:

- 12 ounces semisweet chocolate chips
- ¼ c. milk
- Two T. melted salted butter
- 16 ounces marshmallows
- Apple wedges
- Graham crackers

Directions:

1.   Add wood pellets to your smoker and get your cooker's startup procedure. Preheat your smoker, with your lid closed, until it reaches 450.

2.   Put a cast-iron skillet on your grill and add in the milk and melted butter. Stir together for a minute.

3.   Cover, and let it smoke for five to seven minutes. The marshmallows should be toasted lightly.

4.   Take the skillet off the heat and serve with apple wedges and graham crackers.

Nutrition:

Calories: 90

Carbs: 15g

Fat: 3g

Protein: 1g

32 Bacon Chocolate Chip Cookies

Preparation Time: 10 Minutes

Cooking Time: 30 Minutes

Servings: 24

Ingredients:

- ☐ Eight slices of cooked and crumbled bacon
- ☐ 2 ½ t. apple cider vinegar
- ☐ One t. vanilla
- ☐ Two c. semisweet chocolate chips
- ☐ Two-room temp eggs
- ☐ 1 ½ t. baking soda
- ☐ One c. granulated sugar
- ☐ ½ t. salt
- ☐ Two ¾ c. all-purpose flour
- ☐ One c. light brown sugar
- ☐ 1 ½ stick softened butter

Directions:

1. Mix the flour, baking soda, and salt.

2. Cream the sugar and the butter together. Then lower the speed. Add in the eggs, vinegar, and vanilla.

3.   Still on low, slowly add in the flour mixture, bacon pieces, and chocolate chips.

4.   Add wood pellets to your smoker and follow your cooker's startup method.

5.   Preheat your smoker, with your lid closed, until it reaches 375.

6.   Place some parchment on a baking sheet and drop a teaspoonful of cookie batter on the baking sheet. Let them cook on the grill,

7.   covered, for approximately 12 minutes or until they are browned. Enjoy.

Nutrition:

Calories: 167

Carbs: 21g

Fat: 9g

Protein: 2g

33 Cinnamon Sugar Pumpkin Seeds

Preparation Time: 12 Minutes

Cooking Time: 30 Minutes

Servings: 8-12

Ingredients:

☐ Two T. sugar

☐ seeds from a pumpkin

☐ One t. cinnamon

☐ Two T. melted butter

Directions:

1. Add wood pellets to your smoker and follow your cooker's startup operation. Preheat your smoker, with your lid closed, until it reaches 350.

2. Clean the seeds and toss them in the melted butter. Add them to the sugar and cinnamon. Spread them out on a baking sheet, place on the grill, and smoke for 25 minutes.

3. Serve.

Nutrition:

Calories: 160   Carbs: 5g

Fat: 12g   Protein: 7g

34 Feta Cheese Stuffed Meatballs

Preparation Time: 12 Minutes

Cooking Time: 35 Minutes

Servings: 6

Ingredients:

- Pepper
- Salt
- ¾ c. Feta cheese
- ½ t. thyme
- Two t. chopped oregano
- Zest of one lemon
- One-pound ground pork
- One-pound ground beef
- One T. olive oil

Directions:

1. Place the pepper, salt, thyme, oregano, olive oil, lemon zest, and ground meats into a large bowl.

2. Combine the ingredients thoroughly using your hands.

3. Cut the Feta into little cubes and begin making the meatballs. Take a half tablespoon of

the meat mixture and roll it around a piece of cheese. Continue until all meat has been used.

4.   Add wood pellets to your smoker and follow your cooker's startup procedure.

5.   Preheat your smoker, with your lid closed, until it reaches 350.

6.   Brush the meatballs with more olive oil and put onto the grill. Grill for ten minutes until browned.

Nutrition:

Calories: 390

Carbs: 8g

Fat: 31g

Protein: 20g

35 Butternut Squash

Preparation Time: 30 Minutes

Cooking Time: 2 Hours

Servings: 4-6

Ingredients:

☐ Brown sugar

☐ Maple syrup

☐ 6 T. butter

☐ Butternut squash

Directions:

1. Add wood pellets to your smoker and follow your cooker's startup procedure. Preheat your smoke, with your lid closed, until it reaches 300.

2. Place each half of the squash onto aluminum foil.

3. Increase temperature to 400 and place onto the grill for another 35 minutes.

4. Carefully unwrap each half, making sure to reserve juices in the bottom. Place onto serving platter and drizzle juices over each half. Use a spoon to scoop out and enjoy.

Nutrition:

Calories: 82

Carbs: 22g

Fat: 0g

Protein: 2g

36 Apple Cobbler

Preparation Time: 20 Minutes

Cooking Time: 1 Hour and 30 Minutes

Servings: 8

Ingredients:

- ☐ 8 Granny Smith apples
- ☐ One c. sugar
- ☐ Two eggs
- ☐ Two t. baking powder
- ☐ Two c. plain flour
- ☐ 1 ½ c. sugar

Directions:

1. Peel and quarter apples, place into a bowl. Add in the cinnamon and one c. sugar. Stir well to coat and let it sit for one hour.

2. Add wood pellets to your smoker and follow your cooker's startup form. Preheat your smoker, with your lid closed, until it reaches 350.

3. Place apples into a Dutch oven. Add the crumble mixture on top and drizzle with melted butter.

4. Place on the grill and cook for 50 minutes.

Nutrition:

Calories: 152

Carbs: 26g

Fat: 5g

Protein: 1g

37 Pineapple Cake

Preparation Time: 20 Minutes

Cooking Time: 60 Minutes

Servings: 8

Ingredients:

- One c. sugar
- One T. baking powder
- One c. buttermilk
- Two eggs
- ½ t. salt
- One jar maraschino cherry
- One stick butter, divided
- ¾ c. brown sugar
- One can pineapple slice
- 1 ½ c. flour

Directions:

1. Add wood pellets to your smoker and observe your cooker's startup procedure. Preheat your smoker, with your lid closed, until it reaches 350.

2. Take a medium-sized cast-iron skillet and melt one half stick butter. Be sure to coat the

entire skillet. Sprinkle brown sugar into a cast-iron skillet.

3.   Lay the sliced pineapple on top of the brown sugar. Place a cherry into the middle of each pineapple ring.

4.   Mix the salt, baking powder, flour, and sugar. Add in the eggs; one-half stick melted butter and buttermilk. Whisk to combine.

5.   Put the cake on the grill and cook for an hour.

6.   Take off from the grill and let it sit for ten minutes. Flip onto a serving platter.

Nutrition:

Calories: 165

Carbs: 40g

Fat: 0g

Protein: 1g

38 Ice Cream Bread

Preparation Time: 10 Minutes

Cooking Time: 1 Hour

Servings: 12-16

Ingredients:

☐　1 ½ quart full-fat butter pecan ice cream, softened

☐　One t. salt

☐　Two c. semisweet chocolate chips

☐　One c. sugar

☐　One stick melted butter

☐　Butter, for greasing

☐　4 c. self-rising flour

Directions:

1.　Add wood pellets to your smoker and follow your cooker's startup program. Preheat your smoker, with your lid closed, until it reaches 350.

2.　Set the cake on the grill, cover, and smoke for 50 minutes to an hour. A toothpick should come out clean.

3.　Take the pan off of the grill. For 10 mins., cool the bread.

Nutrition:

Calories: 135

Carbs: 0g

Fat: 0g

Protein: 0g

39 Mediterranean Meatballs

Preparation Time: 15 Minutes

Cooking Time: 35 Minutes

Servings: 8

Ingredients:

- ☐ Pepper
- ☐ Salt
- ☐ One t. vinegar
- ☐ Two T. olive oil
- ☐ Two eggs
- ☐ One chopped onion
- ☐ One soaked slice of bread
- ☐ ½ t. cumin
- ☐ One T. chopped basil
- ☐ 1 ½ T. chopped parsley
- ☐ 2 ½ pounds ground beef

Directions:

1.   Use your hands to combine everything until thoroughly combined. If needed, when forming meatballs, dip your hands into some water. Shape into 12 meatballs.

2.   Add wood pellets to your smoker.

3.   Preheat your smoker, with your lid closed, until it reaches 380.

4.   Place the meatballs onto the grill and cook on all sides for eight minutes. Take off the grill and let sit for five minutes.

5.   Serve with favorite condiments or a salad.

Nutrition:

Calories: 33

Carbs: 6g

Fat: 0g

Protein: 1g

40 Greek Meatballs

Preparation Time: 10 Minutes

Cooking Time: 40 Minutes

Servings: 6

Ingredients:

- ☐ Pepper
- ☐ Salt
- ☐ Two chopped green onions
- ☐ One T. almond flour
- ☐ Two eggs
- ☐ ½ pound ground pork
- ☐ 2 ½ pound ground beef

Directions:

1. Mix all the ingredients using your hands until everything is incorporated evenly. Form mixture into meatballs until all meat is used.

2. Add wood pellets to your smoker and follow your cooker's startup procedure. Preheat your smoker, with your lid closed, until it reaches 380.

3. Brush the meatballs with olive oil and place onto the grill—Cook for ten minutes on all sides.

Nutrition:

Calories: 161

Carbs: 10g

Fat: 6g

Protein: 17g

Conclusion

Now that we've reached the end of the book, I'm very optimistic that you're well-informed about some of the best smoker grilling recipes that will make you a pro at grilling, barbecuing and cooking in general.

You have gotten every secret to cooking with a Wood Pellet Smoker-Grill and you have delicious recipes to try again and again. All you have to do is follow the ingredients and instructions carefully. You have many types of recipes, so you can try a new dish every day and test your cooking skills. Practice will improve your ability to get great flavors from this smoker-grill.

When you put a smoker to the right use and use the best kind of pellets, the induced flavor is so good that not only you but every guest who ends up eating the food is sure to be amazed at the exceptional cooking skills you possess. I put a lot of love, effort and time into this book to make sure every recipe is as good as I wanted it to be.

Of course, as always, most of the recipes allow you to do a little improvising if we assume you are missing some ingredients. However, for best results, we want you to stick to the details as closely as possible.

To start cooking, go through the process of using your Wood Pellet Smoker-Grill and understanding the benefits so that you can use the equipment to its fullest capacity when cooking.

This way, you'll try out different cooking methods, such as smoking, grilling, searing, and more. The instructions are simple, so just follow them as they are presented.

The Wood Pellet Smoker-Grill is much easier than your traditional grills and smokers, so you don't have to worry at all. Just give yourself the initial practice needed to get a full understanding of the functionality of this unit. With regular practice, you will become more confident and comfortable using the smoker-grill to cook a variety of dishes.

So, take advantage of this amazing cookbook and try these recipes to take your taste buds for a real ride.

I hope you enjoy cooking these recipes as much as I enjoyed jotting them down for you. I'm telling you from personal experience: once you get hooked on the BBQ style of cooking, there's no way to stay away from it.

Last but not least, as we said at the beginning of the book, you need to make sure you buy the best kind of smoker and use the perfect pellets, otherwise you will lose the authentic flavor of these perfect recipes. Modify them a bit if you wish, but I think they are as perfect as you would like them to be.

So be prepared to enjoy the beautiful cooking times!

CPSIA information can be obtained
at www.ICGtesting.com
Printed in the USA
BVHW012329150321
602550BV00005B/615